Abyss of Bliss

Poetry to sooth the soul...

NERISSA MARIE

Title Imprint Poetry Books
An imprint of The Quantum Centre, Australia
Published by Happiness Bliss Press
An imprint of The Quantum Centre, Australia

ISBN: 978-0-9946089-8-7

Most Happiness Bliss Press books are available at special quantity discounts for bulk purchase for sales promotions, premiums, fund-raising, and educational needs. For details contact books@happinessbliss.com

National Library of Australia Cataloguing-in-Publication entry
Creator: Marie, Nerissa, author.
Poetry Book - Abyss of Bliss (Love Poems About Life, Poems About Love, Inspirational Poems, Friendship Poems, Romantic Poems, I love You Poems, Poetry Collection, Inspirational Quotes, Poetry Books) / Nerissa Marie.
ISBN: 9780994608987 (paperback)
Subjects: Australian poetry.
Australian poetry -- 21st century.

FIRST EDITION

For Mark.
My guardian angel
who guides the way,
when the sky looks grey.
To a place that's bright
and filled with light.

Contents

Fragile

~ Easy to break, delicate.
Potential to shatter.

I sparkle and shine
lit by the divine,
When the world feels hollow
I'm the one to follow
From the top, the world is a giant rock
a current, a swirl
watch it twist and twirl,
A light in the night
I shine bright
Surrounded by nothing, supported by the ether
I weather storms, of all shapes and forms
A reflection
A resurrection
My light is the spark
hidden in your heart
Let go
There's nothing to follow
You are complete, life is sweet
Release all fear, wipe away your tear
There is nothing but love
I shine this truth from above
illuminating the dark, recesses of your heart
Feel the light within
start to spin
and you'll see you are a star
shining your light upon me from afar

- *Life as a Star*

The death of me
The breath of you
The lofty silence that hangs between those two
The thin cord
The broken record
that lives in my head
of words unsaid
The ego is the one who speaks
before love has reached its peak
The stab of pain
My heart is in flames
I want to kill my mind
so spirit can rule
Why is it 'I' who is so cruel?
You left me long ago
forgot me
I was so shallow
I thought it meant something was wrong with my being
that there was something other than love you were seeing
But I am that
and you am I
It's this beauty that makes me cry
I know it's true
though I cannot see it
For now, I shall simply
grasp
gasp
breathe
till I can feel it

- *Veil*

I took off in flight, disappeared into the night
I ran so far
that's how I got this scar
It runs across my heart and haunts me in the dark
I wanted to forget, but I delved into regret
The reason for our uniting,
had to be more than simply fighting
You showed me the path that I was about to follow
The pool of my life once appeared shallow
I hated everything about you,
wanted to escape the glue that emanates from you
Instead I got stuck
caught in your muck
Now I realise the key, that can set me free
The secret is not to run, it's to let go, have fun
You guided me back here,
to the place that's always been near
Look inside my heart, the true place to start
The scar from afar, looks gloomy and dark
But when you're up close, you can witness the most
It's a crack, there's no doubt about that
When you look inside, it's light you see
You don't have to journey out to sea,
to discover the truth of me
It's bright in here
There never was any fear
I am the love I sought
My heart cannot be bought or sold
that's just a commercial story we've been told
You gave me the key so I could see,
the light that's always glowed within me

- *Haunted by Bliss*

Our relationship makes me frown
It was up, it was down
Driven by fear
Still, I shed a single tear
Remember the good times
that's what they say
Will it take my pain away?
When I was a child
I wasn't wild
You kept me in a cage
Told me the proper way to behave
I tried to be good
Did as you said I should
Till one day I realised, I'd never be free,
trying to be someone better than me
Happiness is found in the moment
not the moments past
or the moments lost
Looking for peace in our past makes our heart cover with frost
The mind has taken control
You've dissolved into the ether
Can I forget? Never
But I can let go
Surrender to the flow
The hands that hold me now, still are not my own
but they are the true hands of home
In the arms of spirit
In the light of peace
I've said my piece
As I acknowledge my sin
it takes me to the place to begin
to unravel

to escape
to happiness
The bubble,
which surrounds my being has popped
The negativity stopped
I am love
That comes from above
and below
wiggling in my toes, and sitting at the tip of my nose
No longer living in fright
I am a holy being of light
The pain you caused
made me become a lost cause
But of course there was a reason for the cause
It opened unseen doors
If I hadn't seen the dark
I'd never have discovered my heart

- *Being of Light*

I am the rose
You are the thorn
You try to keep predators away as I grow
Now I feel all alone
I feel dirty and unworthy
as though I am still the seed, struggling to breathe
To escape, I could wither and die,
merging once more with the sky
dissolving into the air
Will your touch still be there?
As I arch towards the light, your defence has grown in might
My heart attempts to take flight
You've turned your dagger inwards, and now I feel the spike
I know one needs the other to move
But I feel like I've outgrown you
I want to bloom
Not be consumed, in hatred and jealousy
Being guarded as though I am not strong
In nature the thorn knows nothing is wrong
to slow down its grip, but you have taken another trip
I feel suffocated
I want to escape your embrace
But the thorn and the rose wind together
I guess we'll be connected forever
one and the same
You've protected me from being maimed
You're reaching to the heavens with your spike
but I now choose to open my heart,
in full bloom,
to the light

- *Growth*

Each drop of breath
Each drop of blood
We're sucking on something
that asks for nothing
and yet we want more
Forever more
hunting for war
Who will be the first to fall?
Let's kill them all
Each drop of breath
Each drop of blood
We want to fight for the holy throne
and yet we forget we are alone
We emerge from ether
and dissolve into dust
And yet we think to have more is a must
This life is sacred
Our soul naked
Each drop of breath
Each drop of blood
See pure light in your heart
You will die
Don't forget to ask, why?
You're here
because God placed you here
and that is enough
Don't try to act tough
You are forgiven
Spirit has risen
Each drop of breath
Each drop of blood

- *Peace Poem*

We're all fucked
They want to blow us up
Send the men to war
so they can destroy us all
Fear is more damaging than a nuclear bomb,
it's the idea that there is something wrong
The war is on self-awareness
We are being ripped apart
and they want us to stay locked in the dark
Rise with love
Float in bliss
Your peace allows a strong flow of consciousness
I don't want people to die
but like you I've forgotten that we were never born
There's no need to feel forlorn
Find the self
To discover eternal wealth
Act with stealth
The darkness will fall
and you will rise each and every one of us above it all

- *Resistance*

I felt a mother's touch could mend my aching heart
That a part of you could mend the pieces of me
that fell away with string and glue
I wanted you to repair the parts of me that weren't there
self-compassion
confidence
inner acceptance
As though I needed your love to mend me
My heart felt dark and deep
until I let stillness peep
inside
wondering what fears would arise
Only to find the love I need from you
has always lived inside me too

- *Parts of Me*

I tried to be kind
Your cruelty blew my mind
You've cut your cords
with no explanation at all
Because they rejected you
you've shared that burden with me too
I don't want to feel judged
But I know you hold a grudge
I wish I was the perfect woman
then we wouldn't have this problem
I'm sorry
Knowing you don't want the love I can offer
This is all I have to give
All that is left is to forgive
I ask that I am shown
how to love beyond sorrow
So I don't need to wait till tomorrow
to fly into angel's arms
before I discover the peace and love that I am
I really need to feel this now
Quan Yin, all I ask of you is
"Please show me how"

- *Perfect Pain*

I want to lower myself
so you can climb higher
and sit upon a tower
I can shrink
so you can think
that you've made it
reached your goals
I shall stay lower
become a follower
buried beneath your feet
lost in the street
But would it not be easier
if we made the stairs together?
Then we wouldn't have to stop at the top
we could simply dissolve into the ether

\- *Stairway to Light*

Our innocence is broken
through harsh words spoken
The wheel has stopped
We turn to the clock
the imminent tick tock
makes us think this world will never shrink
dissolve into nothing
We all believe in something
That's why we're all messed up
believing the chime is the definition of time
Remove the battery
escape the human factory
Discover the chime
is a lie built from a dime
When the clock sits still
you discover nothing is real
The whisper of grace
takes its place
The gentle ringing
of time singing
is
fake
It's time
for the
planet
to
wake

- *Resurrected Light*

Please like me
Please love me
Please hug me
Like a beggar I ask for you,
wanting you to approve of every little thing I do
I feel broken
Or maybe I've awoken
the parts
that make me feel like everything is falling apart
You've shot a dart, striking my heart
I fear your wrath
I've come unstuck from the glue
that made me think I was good enough for you
I fear you'll hate me, berate me
You've exposed my flaws
Opened my doors
Broken down my walls
Maybe you've done me a favour, opened me wide
so I can take a look about inside
It's all empty, nobody is home
I am the one sitting upon the judgement throne
Through the pain, the endless game
you've shown me how to look through every cranny and nook
To see what we can be when we throw away the key,
eternally free

- *Diary of Bliss*

I miss you so much
Long for your touch
Your sweet voice, makes me feel there's nothing to be
that I am enough for reality
When times get tough
I long for you
to get me unstuck from this mental glue
Life feels so hollow
It's you I want to follow,
into the ocean of ether
Where I don't have to feel emotional weather
Come and fix the broken parts
Please let's start with my heart
How could you just disappear?
Dissolve into the atmosphere?
Sometimes life feels so real
I pray, I kneel
surrender to the divine
Please take my pain, I know it's not mine
I wake up
I lose touch
Dancing back and forth
Trying to do my best
Life is the ultimate test
No matter what cards we're dealt
in the end we all melt
Folding back into the seams
Dissipating into the dream
Who am I then?
This person, this being
Is there any truth in what I'm seeing?
I believe in you

and that helps me dissolve the glue
I see the immortal drops of sand, we each hold in hand
I'm not this body, this form
You've gifted me this truth
Letting go, stepping into the flow
We are spirit, swirling in the mist
beings of bliss
My heart starts to swell
I know you're my guardian angel
A lifetime, passes in an instant
I am grateful for this moment, to be present
It won't be long, till I sit with you
watching over those, I love too…

- *Immortal Sand*

Suicide is a ride
It strips away my pride
Letting go of reality
it shatters my destiny, and affirms there is no one less than me
There is nothing to fight, I give up all right,
to be somebody
as I am willing to sacrifice my body
Awaken and become free,
that's where I want to be
I need to surrender to the story untold
Let my mind be a reflection of spirits light
Please let my heart take flight
I give my fears not to the night,
I hand them over to the light
In darkness and despair, always a light glows there
I flicker in the night
A connection to infinite light so bright it shatters my soul,
I am born from source, as I kill my minds remorse
We are not this body, this soul,
the stories untold
We are words written by spirit
I choose to trust the hands that wrote this script
I am not the creator of my manuscript
I still want to die
But the spark inside me knows it's time to fly

- *Silent Flight*

I don't want you to die
the thought makes me cry
Will I ever be ready to say goodbye?
I know that when you leave
a part of me will grieve
But a deeper part,
locked in my heart,
knows this is just the start
of a deeper love
not bound
not found
not hidden
not written
A love that goes beyond the sea
Further than you and I can see
Sometimes I pretend it's you and me
But as I realise oneness
together,
forever,
we are set free

- *Heart Knots*

Feel the fire in your belly, as you turn off the telly
The screen is now blank, you're driving the tank
Seek reality by turning within, this is the only place to begin
Once trapped inside a box, you've discovered the lock
Forget about your troubles, they don't exist
You are a mirror of pure consciousness, divine bliss
Hand your life over to source,
the petrol behind your driving force
Be governed by your heart,
not images of destruction and desolate
You are home when you watch within and discover the place
that you begin

- *One Spark*

I think I'm in control of my life
but God's the one who holds the knife
How can I manipulate my role,
when I'm not even sure if I own my own soul?
On Earth it's not a permanent stay
Maybe we've come here to play
It feels like:

pleasure

pressure

pain

Is there anything to gain?
I'm wearing a mask
in this giant farce
One day I'll be dead
who knows if this poem will ever be read
I feel ashamed
My soul is maimed
I'm limping through time
trying to create this rhyme

illusion

delusion

confusion

When life feels like a test, because everything's a mess
There's nothing left, you may as well set your mind to rest

unwind

rewind

witness mankind

an ants nest of chatter
Watch the world unfold, it doesn't matter
We are not who we think we are
We manifest as babies from places afar

Unlock the ego,
forgiveness releases pain and ends all sorrow
There is only today
Stop the mind whirlwind, and let consciousness begin
You're not really here, there's nothing to fear
You are nothing but love
witnessing
manifesting
creating
this whole drama from above

- *Tranquil Clarity*

I won't let the dark side win
I won't let it think it's something
We're all so scared and we feel unprepared
But when death takes us,
will the dark escape us?
We try to run
Forget, have fun
Frolic in the sun
But evil stories have already been spun
ebbing their way into our thoughts
Caught on the edge of webs
we all feel trapped
and yet we want to please
this evil disease
Spreading throughout the world
a manmade machine
We need to accept the darkness that lives
Take away its space to breathe
Retrieve our sacred innocence
Forgetting we are less than the silken smoothness of a baby's bum
we allow the beat of evil's drum
to think it owns us
We allow ourselves to be possessed
Blaming ourselves for creating this mess
"No more!"
I shout my dark thoughts to the wall
"Get out you clouts"
You thought that you could programme me?
Well you never saw this coming
This is the day you thought you'd never see
Now you are the ones running
A new beat is drumming

You created this machine driven by light
One brave soul who is not afraid of the night
I am evil
I am love
And this is what grants powers not from above
You destroyed my soul
I looked inside only to find that all you took was never mine
I am taking my power back
and bringing forth an army of angels
For you are only light
and this is the knowledge that shall destroy your pain
The darkness is dead
You only lived in my head
I know you're not real
You never were a big deal
You thought I'd never come
But you forgot
I am the drum
This avalanche of light has only just begun

- *Aro of Light*

Tenderness

~ Gentle touch required.
Sensitive to pain.

In the palm of your hand
lies a distant land
Hidden from view, created by you
You've become a player, in this world of maya
Trapped in the net
we all forget
the distant shore
isn't real at all
The place beyond
where you've forgotten you originate from
Life feels so real
Everyone thinks it's a big deal
If we evaporate when we die
maybe everything is a lie
Search for freedom,
that's your kingdom
We were right about something,
life isn't for nothing
Through the shadows let stillness peep
into your heart, embrace it deep
Rise from the sleep
Go back home
Remember you're never alone
You create the world
It's one swirl
Created with dust
Formed by lust
Desire and greed are not what we need
Discover the seed,
watch it breathe

- *Distant Worlds*

Consciousness is simmering,
life is glimmering
The shadows that lived in my heart are starting to fall apart
I lived in the dark
Thinking it was the safest place to park
the pieces of me I never wanted to see
But now the light is coming in
illuminating all that I've hidden
The darkest thoughts that I believed were forbidden
I tried to ban the parts of myself,
that I felt were unworthy of universal wealth
The flame has crept inside my brain
It lit in stillness,
when I felt my pain
The things I thought were bad
the pieces that made me sad
taught me gratitude
The light behind the mind
The peace behind the bliss
The parts of me I didn't want to see
are the parts that are there to set us free
The light of the heart, drives away the dark
The love of the soul, of the fears untold
break the mould which tries to hold,
onto the pieces of you,
you wish weren't true
Trust that you are brighter than a star
You are the light that dissolves the blackest night
Your guilt and shame is part of the game
You are already free,
because you exist you are more than enough for reality

- *Love of Light*

Open my heart
Split me apart
Eat me whole
Swallow my soul
Do I taste like soup? Or a pile of goop?
I want to taste sweet, a real treat
Like the nectar of God
Am I made of spirit?
They say it's so
If you taste me, you will see
what has made me reality
If I lived on a throne,
would I taste of more than flesh and bone?
Maybe my fibre is beyond this body
Am I somebody?
Something?
Where do I begin
to unravel my soul?
To unlearn what I've been told?
If my soul isn't meat
then how do I meet
the real me deep inside?
Please help me
uncover
unravel
the form
where I think I'm from
Learn to travel, beyond the flesh
Become unstuck from this mesh
I'm not even real
I know I'd make a lovely meal

- *God's Dinner*

The eye of the butterfly
never shifts, never sways
The caterpillar calls
to fly above it all
You first need to shield life's monsoons,
cocoon
Find nest to rest, a sacred place to invest
Healing comes from pain undone
Thus the web is spun
The eye blinks
So much time spent in darkness
So much time spent in pain
So much time longing to breathe yet again
Lying still in your bed, you never moved
not even to reach for a piece of bread
But the eye kept watching
Silence haunts
Fear of being hunted
Suspended in the dark
A hanged man
You emerge
your soul has torn apart
and in its place you find two wings,
simple things, fluttering
And your eyes they have never wavered
looking deep within
You escape into the light, and once more take flight
Your eye always remained the same
I look for that 'I'
as I too struggle, before I fly

- *Eye of the Butterfly*

Escape the haze,
created by the minds maze
Those you fear, are only here
because the scared part of your soul allows them near
Everyone is a guest in your reality
even your own family
Let everything melt
Forgive the cards you've been dealt
Close your eyes
Watch the demise
of the reality you thought to be true,
as you discover you're not even you
Rest your head, soul, body and breath
Feel the illusion, acknowledge the conclusion
You're made by the magic of love
Not created by a man above
Everyone you meet, it's you, you greet
Open your eyes,
unveil the disguise
Fear shuts down our heart,
the only place to start
Take a bird's eye view
Watch the pain controlling you
Ask, who am I?
Follow the last breath
Let your soul rest
Feel the happiness within
Let your heart swim
In the ocean, like a droplet you fall,
as you merge with all
For you are the one sending blessings from above
A spark of the divine

I am you, you are mine
Everything, everyone, is sublime
Nature holds the key to dissolve reality
Sacred breath helps trees to grow
In your heart discover it's true,
the divine breathes through you

- *Divine Breath*

What is it that you don't have, that makes you feel so bad?
Strip the illusion
Escape the confusion
Through your eyes you see a reality,
that forgets your majesty
You see that you are incomplete
as you look outside and attempt to compete
The cycle of birth and death plays on repeat
You're awake and yet you are dead
Get out of your head
Did you really remember to climb out of bed?
What is it that you see, that makes you so sure of the
permanence of reality?
Ocean waves hit the shore,
then disappear as though they never existed at all
Learn to swim through waves of compassion
For your body and soul, the heart of you,
is made of water too

- *Pure Awareness*

I see Gods light burning in you
This desire to know truth burns in few
Become the fire
Swallow your hearts desire
Forget the web
Find the spider
who masterfully makes you desire
On whose bridge does he sit?
And where from comes the web?
Is this world real?
Or is it all a trap in your head?
The spider is ego
The web illusion
And you are trapped in the dust of confusion
With pincers the spider sucks
the fly who got caught in his muck
Duck and dive
Come out alive
Free the nest
Swim in the world
Fly through the sky
Die
Try
Forget all
This is the hearts call
Escape
Recreate
Give your life to spirit
Dissolve into bliss
You are consciousness
The spider and web are you
Who knows this?

Very few
It's one thing to speak
but this makes us weak
Forget to try
and you shall fly
out of the shadows
into the ether
Shift your desired direction
become the reflection

- *Error of Perception*

Our skin is a shell
that makes one person believe another belongs in hell
But you are not the skin
You are no-thing
Forget who you think you are
Look to your heart to illuminate the dark
Forget religion or race
We are all made of grace

- *Merge into That*

Be who you are
you know you'll go far

It's okay to have it tough
It's okay to feel not enough
It's okay to live rough
Dissolve the glass screen
For when life's curtain shatters at the seams
we see the first thread of the dream

- *Breath of Light*

Were you made?
How deep is your grave?
Are you dead?
Or is it simply the fears in your head
that are manipulating you,
telling you what to do?
The beauty that beats within you
The light of the sun, from whence your heart is spun
is the true source of the drum

- *Pure*

When the divine wanted to make you mine
starbursts exploded in my head
I loved taking you to bed
Then I realised I could never own you
or disown you
I wondered if I could borrow you for a moment longer
like a worn out library book
Could I not return you
or would they make me pay a fee?
I guess that's okay with me
But before we get closer
we need to be torn apart
So that we can discover the true beat of our heart
I want to own you
To come back to you
life and life again
But this life is full of pain
and this lifetime I am immortally maimed
So next time we part
let's not look for others
let's dissolve into the heart
Then the universes offer of joining us
will not be like a library
for we shall never be apart

- *Borrowed*

Demons have created a wall
one we cannot pierce at all
They don't want the psychics to see,
their plans
They've created a way
to suck away the stars so bright
so we can only see night
When you try to tune in
they know you are listening
Remote viewers are coming to visit
but they are unwelcome, turn them away from your home
Let them find another place to roam
We want to know what they'll do next
There is nothing you need to see
Nothing you need to be
They are keeping themselves locked behind closed doors
Pretending they never existed at all
But there are some who know
that the humans wrestle with more than minds
That is why we must throw down our weapons
surrender to the divine
For you are here as a guide
A person whom no one understands
and yet you're expected to feel comfortable around man
Forsake your fear
lend an ear
to the hearts that shatter like stars of glass
Living deluded by this giant farce
For the demons do not know
that tomorrow,
never existed
We have resisted

and now we will take them out
They have built their own walls and can't escape
Send them your prayers
Forgive their aims
Release the need to be a slave
Send your mind to the grave
Emerge reborn
Emerge as jnana
The true purpose of human existence
is not dedicated persistence
it's letting go
Allow spirit to swallow, you
So you can merge with the demons too
and unlock the suffering of this world
As they are blinded by the light
that once more has come
to rule the night

- *Ignited*

We are all being called to war
Put down your weapons
There is no need to fight at all
Sit in bliss
Illuminate your consciousness
Your light is the power
Let your soul bloom like a flower
The light is here
watch the fear run
The war has just begun
Douse them in flames
The suffering of your heart is where you're maimed
Allow yourself to heal
Nothing is real
Learn to feel
When humanity realises we are all made of love
there will no longer be need for blessings from above
The world is hollow as we travel like sheep
Doing the bidding of the ones, we cannot see
Forgetting we are already free
Illuminate your mind
You are the salvation of mankind
I bow to your grace
I thank your ability to light this place

- *Unravel Grace*

Judgement and blame is a messed up game
Designed to kill the mind and let fear rule sublime
Swallow your pain
Don't let it drain, the sparkle of love
the seed of you that is present in all beings too
Guilt is used to manipulate
so we can all learn to feed off hate
Blaming the ones filled with hatred and greed in times of need
keeps us stuck, in illusional muck
You are a tree, weak at the knees
Because you think you need to feed off jealousy,
take heed
The one who points, shoots three fingers in his direction
It's time for a resurrection
Self-awareness, the place from which you've sprung,
is the seed of light where it all begun
Put down your weapons, of judgement and blame
let's start a new game, of forgiveness,
rebirth
Resurface from the earth
acknowledging that which you are,
the light inside the star

- *Shine*

Before you disappear, it's time to dissolve your fear
You're waiting for God to appear
He's already here
Deep in your heart, lies the key
The answers you need to set yourself free,
and dissolve reality
It's time to be brave
as you face the grave
It's time to wake
Release all hate
It's not about tomorrow
or embracing sorrow
We all have regret
So let's forgive and forget
Can't hold on any longer
You're growing stronger,
as your body slips away
into the disarray
Surrender to spirits kiss
We are watching as you drift, back home to bliss

- *Leaving Earth*

Nestled in the arms of our creator
we cry, "see you later!"
Diving into the unknown
we forget our origin
Becoming obsessed with foragin'
For this and that and maybe a new hat
Life gets glum
We begin to feel dumb
Fear is an illusion
This whole world a delusion
Realise the source
The place the soul rests of course
Connected to the ether
Neglected never
Only we've forgotten who we are
The source of the 'I'
The path is within
Our origin
Diving back into creation

- *Diving Deep*

I was a child when my heart began to beat
Someone told me what it did and where it lived
Then I heard a thunderous sound and felt the swell
the pure place where consciousness likes to dwell
It was awareness that made it start
Before that I lived in grace
with no need for a heart

- *Life's Embrace*

Devotion

~ A pathway of total surrender

My body is a vessel
Spirit the mortar and pestle
You cannot crush me
I am already free
It's just a matter of dissolving reality
A spice is malleable,
that doesn't make it any less valuable
I am open to change,
for life to rearrange
The structure you've clung to,
doesn't define you
I surrender my soul, to a story untold
Life is divine, I am but a speck amongst mankind
Sometimes I feel small, like I have no worth at all
I am the wind,
the grass,
the being,
the mask
I take God's hand,
as I rediscover
I AM

- *Trust*

You are perfect
You are divine
You are infinitely sublime
I give my life to you
What else is there to do?
Sometimes I hate myself and feel like I'm living in hell
So I hand this over to you God, and I know all is well
Can I transcend these ropes that bind my mind?
Can I transcend the idea that I am part of humankind?
Am I a part
a piece
a fragment
of this place?
Am I really part of the human race?
Sometimes I despise my culture
how we bully and devour each other like vultures
But I know in the present, that life is a mirage
A mirror of divinity reflecting the eyes of God
So I hand over the key to God, the creator of my reality
You created me
but I can set myself free
When I recognise I am you
together we dissolve the glue
that kept us together and apart
My heart is open
I give my life to you
Thank you God, for thinking of creating me too
I am so honoured to be,
a part
a piece
a fragment of you

- *Transcendence*

I feel so lost
My brain is starting to defrost
It's all a lie
Everybody is high
There is no reason, for the change in season
Look at the sky, watch it flash by
We never die and yet we wonder, why?
What is the purpose?
It's rising to the surface
the being of you
the creation of me
God please set me free
Allow me to see
This is my call
Show me God that is all
I need to know, why this place feels hollow
Find the seer
I know it's near
That'll be the end
Am I going round the bend?
Or tapping into truth that'll dissolve the spoof?
Love is the master
the truth that I'm after
Nothing is as it seems
This world is a dream
There is no need for warm weather,
as we surrender to the ether
The spark of the seed
The truth indeed

- *Love is God*

Show me God
Show me God
Show me God
I'm letting go of
this me, this she, this he
Let me live from the heart
Unveil the mask that traps me in the dark
Why do I feel in pain?
Will God make it go away?
If God is in me, why can't I see?
I don't understand
the purpose of God's plan
I need faith
To trust in this place
I feel hollow
Need to forget tomorrow
Forget myself
Uncover the self
From where do I arise?
Will this question lead to my demise?
I am starting to despise,
my mind
But I feel I need to be kind
There is nothing left to say
No other words to get in the way
Show me God
Show me God
Show me God

- *Divine Grace*

The waves lap the ocean shore,
dissolving into sand forever more
Sink or swim
We swallow the bubble of oxygen
which merges us with the ocean of life
Yet from where comes this bubble?
Air or ether
Will we ride upon the shoreline forever?
Or dissolve into the ocean shore
and be free forever more?

- *Surrender to Sea*

It's a great fate indeed, not to be driven by fear or greed

I'm all alone
Nobody is home
I have no fear
Nobody is here
I realise the 'I'
that masks the disguise,
that I originally thought
made me alive
There is no me
I am nobody
I am already free
You think you're you
But we are one not two
The 'I' likes to talk
I like this
I am happy
I am sad
This 'I' it likes to think it's me
But I am nothing but reality
Nothing is me
Nothing is you
My ego fights to be something
But what it wants to be, causes pain in my reality
I want to be good
Act as others think I should
But I'm living in an illusion,
so trying to *be* creates confusion
I need to be naked,
connect to something sacred
Dissolve into the ego

Let it all go
Get out of my mind
I am running around blind
Thinking I'm something,
when really I'm nothing
The pain is hidden in the thing
Forget all, hear the call,
of surrounding bliss, pure consciousness
Unleash the shackles that bind me tight
The idea that I need to do everything right
Swallow the key
Set myself free

- *Dissolving*

You are a radiant light in a world of darkness
that many may want to harness
You are all
Hear spirits call
Forget not enough
Your spirit is tough
made from love
Your presence is a gift from angels above

- *Presence*

Life is so magical and full of grace
I have never sat in such a happy place
I have learnt not to be unhappy that I'm unhappy
I do not know how to manifest air
So why should I have a care?
For so long my mind has defined my destiny
I forgot the core of me
eternal bliss
No beginning, no end
I allow spirit to send
the arc of light that makes me move
right through my body
I surrender to that, the eternal sunbeam
life as a dream
We are but shadows of light
dancing in the night
Swallowed by fear
Thinking we are here
Starving for faith
Forgetting we are reflections of grace
With a splash we disappear
I sit and wait for God to appear
Never realising he is already here
Hidden in our real nature
Surrender to the call
Realise you were never here at all

- *Disappearing*

Angel Guide
Thank you for always being by my side
for coming along for the ride
You'll be my best friend,
right till the end
You show me the way to turn,
and good habits to learn
I am so grateful for your company
Your healing sets me free
You always glow
with the wisdom of one who knows
You're up to date,
never late
You know the way home,
back to my heart
Learning to follow your intuitive guidance is an easy art,
as your voice always leads back to my heart
Thank you dear one, you are so much fun!

- *United by Grace*

The walls we build to protect ourselves from the storm,
don't let anything in at all
Inside it's
cold
damp
dank
Who knew how much we strove to protect ourselves
would create a place so hard and cold it stank
Till we look within we are all trapped
Look and you shall discover a place of love so pure
the walls you built will dissolve into something less obscure
Maybe they never existed
and you are already sitting where it's warm
Wrapped in divine love
Sheltered from the storm

- Sacred Shelter

Whilst you think you are you
God exists too
That's why it's okay
to ask God to take your fears away

The stream is a dream
The thought is bare
Discovering who you are, rare
Your mind is the cause of all resistance,
break through with persistence
Watch repetitive thoughts, the cycle of pain
Forgive your heart
It's the ego that likes to hurt and maim
Dive deep
Start at the beginning
you're swimming
in a dream it would seem
Nothing is what it seems

- *Love is All*

Come and spread your wings
and see that you are a being of positivity
We lose vital chi, when we focus upon negativity
Spread your wings and fly,
up into a diamond lit sky

- *Portal*

You light the dark
An infinite spark
Oh how you glow
Filling the cracks that feel hollow
You're a messenger of the divine
You are sublime
You light the way
so we can see
what it is to be free
You're nothing but bliss
A ripple across the ocean of infinite consciousness
I salute the light
Surrender my soul
I watch my heart
release fears of the dark
To the story untold
The abyss of gold

-

Abyss of Bliss

In Love

~ Discovering the divinity of the self,
our true nature.

In bliss,
we realise nothings amiss
There is nothing to fear
Love is already here
We are the light
that shines so bright
The one we seek
Take a step back
look for a crack
Nothing is real, it's all surreal
The air; I'll let you in on a secret, nothing is there
It's all a dream
Shift the screen,
you are the abyss
The place you miss
Illuminated bliss

- *Bliss*

Open your eyes
allowing the lashes to brush one another
top to bottom
Their soft embrace makes your body look half awake
and yet you see
what is yet unseen
the veil between the screen
When your eyes are tight shut
you see nothing much
but open them slight
to see a horizon of light
The darkness is there
but until the pictures of the world fill the void
you are left devoid
of
scene
scenery
dreamily
you wake
Allow consciousness to burn
the embers of fire
your hearts desire
To discover the source
of light
silhouetted against the night

- *Fire Horizon*

You are a reflection on the lake of God
One that cannot be pulled from the water with a rod
Love is the divine nature of the human spirit
Yet we cannot see it, nor hear it
So we must learn to feel it
Look to see the eyes that have projected you
This is the 'I' that you are a piece of too
Is there one?
Or is there two?
The lake ripples
Yet the eyes of your creator stay stable
the heartbeat of this fable
Throw a rock into the lake
It's time for your projection to wake

- *Ripple*

To hate yourself is the greatest sin
For where on Earth do you begin?
You start at the source of course,
behind the fear, the failure, the lack, the remorse
You are the bliss,
that dissolves the abyss
I am you
You am I
You are God
made in the image of man
Remember where you began
This place is mad
That's why everyone is so sad,
wishing for things they never had
Trying to be
something
someone
somebody
You are already the reality
This place is a dream
Nothing is what it seems
Take my hand
Surrender to God's plan
Embrace the fact that you're here,
and everything feels so near
It all feels so real, it's surreal
The spark inside illuminates,
the dark that resides inside your brain
You are no bigger than a piece of grain
A puppet in the hands of spirit
I know you can hear it
the gentle call

behind the wall
of your mind,
unwind
You are divine
There is peace for you,
on this planet too
God designed it especially for you
And you are one with all that is
You are the breath of the poet
Deep inside I know you know it
Forget heavens call
There is no wall
Maybe you don't exist at all
But if you do,
it's because God,
fell
in
love
with
you

- *Universe Romance*

I thought there was a lake
Upon which God's eyes bathed
The eyes watched me swimming in the stream
Then the eyes took me over and this all became a dream
There is no lake, no stream,
I am not a reflection in God's dream
I don't exist
There is no need to persist
in looking for me
I am already free
There is nothing
I am that
My ego is the hook
My brain the crook
that has robbed me of nothing
Although I think they've stolen something
There never was any lake
Now I am awake

- *Floating*

If your mind didn't exist
you wouldn't be here

"There is no word for the silence within."
So my guru said
I took this thought to bed
Feeling a state of love so deep,
I fell asleep
Upon awakening,
all conscious thought began breaking
Love, Consciousness, Bliss
The desire for peace has led me to this moment,
God's kiss
Relationships are projections of the mind
Release all thought, surrender, unwind
So it would seem,
that every thought,
experience,
voice
is all but a dream
Silence within is the place from which,
the truth of life shall begin

- *The Silence Within*

One beat
Love
One drum
Love
One giant thrum
Love
The heart of creation brings peace to a nation
The universal sound reverberating through town
How can we hear a sound that isn't playing to our ear?
Light is the source
Aum the first sound
Bringing this party to town
Relax the ego
Surrender the soul
Lose control
Then you'll hear it start
the music that plays from the heart
It lifts your feet from the ground
and makes us walk and talk to a new beat
When it hits the street
as people start to listen
you'll see their aura begin to glisten
Its dust and love
A song from the angels above
The more who listen the louder it grows
The rhythm of creation unites the nation
With one heart listen to the beat
You can hear it in the street

- Glisten

Divine peace is found
when we recognise the place from which we've sprung,
is the same place from which we all began
Illuminated beings thinking we're individuals
We are illusions of the mind
All fighting for the belief that we are
objects,
beings,
mankind
But are we kind or are we cruel?
Using consciousness as a tool,
create a veil,
sail across the sea
Realise you begin at the start
From true love you never part

- *Seeker's Silence*

Put the world away
Leave it for a rainy day
These words are not made to be sold
This story is not meant to be told
The world is a toy
A great ploy
You think it's part of you
When really you are part of it too
Forget that you are here
Forget your every fear
Give up you
Give up 'I'
Don't ask why
Just escape this place where you think you belong
It's not where you originate from
Well it is
and it isn't
Can you feel it?
Merge into the light
that dwells inside your third eye
The place from which you arise
Which is already here
now
present
presenting you
Touch the screen
Dissolve the dream

- *Immersion*

The dynamite that dissolves all fright
is discovering your consciousness manifest as bliss
Purity itself
To identify with the body is to suffer
Divine love is the buffer
We want protection
But as soon as we are born we start to die
Time flashes by
We all look for the map that will take us back
to source
to love
to innocence
There is nothing to change
Nothing to rearrange
You are the map
That can take you back
To bliss
For you never travelled anywhere
You are already consciousness

- *Home*

I lay on the floor
my heart soared
Caught in that place, between
emptiness and grace,
ether and emptiness
The press of the Earth, makes us crave rebirth
But the hearts song, is what shows us we belong
Caught in the gap
ready to let go of all
discover the truth of life
God created this wall
"Let's tear it down."
"Can you find the bricks?"
"What's that you say? They're not even here?"
"My word, I never realised God was so near."

- *Bewildered*

I feel such a blessing
such an undeniable grace
When I sit in the place
where I looked upon your face
The magic in you, is filling me up too
Thank you for your surrender
It has helped me remember
that light,
that space,
that grace of the heart
Tears wet my eyes
As spirit unveils her disguise
There is nothing but love
Before its time for me to leave
I am set free
The heavens above
have opened their door
I am surrounded by peace, forever more

- *Magic in You*

Who looks through my eyes?
The seer that's who
The same one who lives
inside you

You are nothing but a ball of bliss
Floating through the abyss
You think you're here
That's why you're full of fear
But you're not really there
You could be anywhere
You're a special soul, or so I'm told
by the angels watching your life unfold
You think you have to do something bold
to be worthy of life
But you are worthy because you exist
You're a starburst of bliss,
floating through the abyss

- *Starburst*

Open your heart, you are an angel sent by the divine,
to experience what it's like to live amongst mankind
A kingdom of angels who've forgotten the way
to heaven's gates, which are open today
Stop for a moment,
listen, breathe
Let the mind be still
and discover the secret of free will
There is nothing to gain,
desire brings suffering and pain
Be as slow as a snail, to remove the veil
The light beyond
the distant shore
that is our front door
Love, light and bliss
Nothing's amiss
We think it so
Until we know
we're beings of love,
of ether and fairy dust
We are the light,
consciousness itself
The ocean of love is our true home
We're already there
The thread is unravelling
and we are travelling
to a place so close
it's a wonder we haven't noticed before,
we are already at heaven's door

- *Eternal Angel*

I felt the light
shine so bright,
it hit my third eye
glistening like a sun in the sky
My brain blew open
I thought it was broken
Everything went white
I felt only love
To get to this place, to feel God's grace
I let myself acknowledge the sorrow
Didn't leave it till tomorrow
Witnessed who I am
The divine exploded my mind with a bam
I thought I would blow
as I allowed the light to follow
Met the bridge of death it's a nice place to be
it set me free
I've become an addict of,

love

light

bliss

Searching once more when I became grounded,
for pure consciousness
It wasn't till later
I realised the light wasn't real
I had to go behind the mind
to see what was there
You are beautiful
You are valuable
The one you seek
is the permanent substratum of all that exists

- *Divine Explosion*

Life isn't all it seems
A jumble of dreams
The ego, leaves us hollow
So we don't know where to turn, or who to follow
Trying to prove, we are better than the rest
We get into the groove, of putting our mind to the test
Take it slow
There is nowhere to go
You are the creator
not a dominator
We try to dictate
Attempt to create
A life of achievement
a universal dent
You are already complete
There is no need to compete
The wires in your brain have crossed
it's why you feel so lost
Release control
the effort to be an independent soul
All hearts are connected,
infinitely protected
We are one with all,
can never fall
We think we need to BE,
cannot see
We are everything and nothing
Travel the road home
Return to the twilight zone
Stop, even for a moment, and you will see
when you sit and just be
you dissolve reality

The 'I' merges with the divine
there is no mine
only the infinite sublime
Surrender all
You hear the call
of the place within
dive in, swim
Let the current take you
No one can make you
Forget who you are
Discover you're a star
Peace and love doesn't come from above
it's in your heart
the true place to start
Rise anew
released from the glue
You're not the mind
Unwind
You've reached the peak
You are what you seek
Love consciousness and bliss
the light of the abyss

- *Life Beams*

The world exists because you think it into creation every time you wake in the morning

The Poetry

Abyss of Bliss, was written as I drifted between worlds. Between dreaming and awakening. Becoming conscious, that life is not all it seems. That everyone is real and yet they are illusions projected by the smorgasbord of the mind.

It's my love letter to you. Written with desperation, hope and love. Searching for meaning and presence. Discovering the only truth worth trusting is buried in the heart.

Pain, rejection and unity immerses us in the soup of divinity together as one forever. I would be delighted to delete my mind and everything in it. Just as a broken lover desires to escape the pain of separation. However, I'd be even more delighted to see myself living inside the heart of all beings. For you to discover that the love hidden inside of you is what heals your soul, this world, and existence itself. It is all you seek. Follow the mind back to the place it arises from, the heart.

Each day I wait with trepidation and excitement before the arms of death, or I could say eternal life. Wondering, when I cross to the other side will cars, houses and trinkets be of value? I highly doubt it, and that makes me perceive a ruined society. We are all searching for treasure in empty places. The caress of a lover can never be forgotten and neither can our true nature, bliss. I refuse to allow hatred to butter my

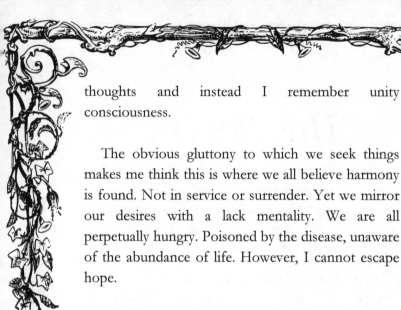

thoughts and instead I remember unity consciousness.

The obvious gluttony to which we seek things makes me think this is where we all believe harmony is found. Not in service or surrender. Yet we mirror our desires with a lack mentality. We are all perpetually hungry. Poisoned by the disease, unaware of the abundance of life. However, I cannot escape hope.

Will the amount I feed the poor or nurture the less fortunate be valued after death? It seems more likely. Or will these traumas fold themselves into the consciousness of life and death only to be forgotten by my mind as I depart this world?

Human feelings are often so overwhelming that we lose our sense of purpose and place. We forget to question, what are we doing here? Why do we exist? Instead we become lost in the human experience. Losing track of time, becoming consumed by our external world.

Hatred, fear and jealousy manifest through seeking outside the core to discover the real you. Let go of all expectations. Go beyond your external world. Just for a moment.

Life can surface emotions of pleasure and pain. Guilt, regret, shame and lack often haunt our soul. *Abyss of Bliss,* looks beyond emotion, beyond form,

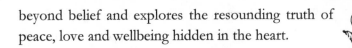

beyond belief and explores the resounding truth of peace, love and wellbeing hidden in the heart.

True reality is found buried in the chest. The true treasure chest. Filled with golden light, and bliss. Love is not a destination, it's not a feeling, it's not a relationship, it is what you are. You don't have to seek it out, you just need to escape the minds lies so that you can see your being, naked and true.

I promise that if you look beneath your skin, through your bones, beneath your fears, and beneath your thoughts you'll discover the most blissful nothingness that will set you free for eternity. When the mind is silent, we discover divine love, our true nature.

Our heart holds the key to going beyond the mind and discovering a new destiny. Where we surrender all of our problems to the universe and rediscover the beauty behind the veil. Dissolving into a consciousness of wellbeing and soul harmony. You are valuable. You are a gift to the world and you are important. You are loved, and all is well.

May you walk in light, and discover that no matter where you come from or where you've been you are a manifestation of divinity. Worthy of love, worthy of joy and peace. Something miraculous and magical has made you manifest, of which you are a part. Not separate, not different from, but completely, wholly, blessed and adored by and part of.

We are nothing more than beams of light floating through consciousness. Projecting desires in the abyss. All the while forgetting we are pure, simple, humble manifestations of bliss.

With all my heart.

With all my love.

Peace Peace Peace.

Poetry Index

About the Poet

Nerissa Marie, loves sharing light and love throughout the universe. She sends blessings and smiles to all who surround her. Nerissa Marie is an author, naturopath, and mystic. She believes all beings are equal, sacred manifestations of the divine and that when we recognise the divinity within all beings, including ourselves we create a pathway to inner-peace and a harmonious planet.

Life is a journey and all emotions and experiences; pain, despair, failure, success, joy, happiness are healing tools guiding us deeper within ourselves until we discover the source of our true being, bliss and love. She looks forward to meeting you on the journey to sacred union and to the awakening of humanity as all hearts unite in infinite peace.

Her goal is to serve universal spirit, and realise eternal love. A few of Nerissa Marie's favourite things include crystals, meditation, fairies and cherry smoothies. She has an immense amount of gratitude, to be living on planet earth and for the intertwining of her reader's spirits, on the dance of life, as she shares her heart through the written word.

Namaste.

NerissaMarie.com

Inspirational Books by Nerissa Marie

Available on Amazon and most other retailers in Hardcover, Paperback, Kindle and Epub format.

Peace, Love and You is a self-help, spiritual guidebook that empowers you to look at the true nature of your being; divine love, compassion, and bliss. You are perfect, whole and complete simply because you exist. You are a divine expression of love. Peace, Love and You is an inspirational book that aims to empower your soul with inner wisdom.

When fate hands you the perfect woman, it's easy to know what to do. For Hugo de La Laville, life's a little more complicated. He has three perfect, potential fiancées…
Paris Mafia Princess, explores the time we waste on trying to get even and finding the right partner at all costs. How our natural competitive instinct can be used constructively, and why we sometimes forget that the most important relationship we have in life is the one we develop within ourself.

Princess Kate, loves to meditate. One day deep in bliss, she levitates high into the sky, leaving behind her friends and family. Prince Ravi Yogi arrives at the kingdom, offering to help bring Princess Kate back down to Earth. Will they listen to his advice? Or will Princess Kate, forever float above the palace, just out of reach?
This books intention is to build your child's self-esteem through a story of mindfulness meditation.

FREE GIFTS! Future releases, free book promotions, and more!
Available at **NerissaMarie.com**